Contents

KV-676-660

Preface

This book is designed to introduce pupils to the fundamentals of web publishing using Microsoft FrontPage Express.

The book is based on the "Exchanging and Sharing Information" and "Developing Ideas and Making Things Happen" objectives for Year 8 found within the **'Framework for teaching ICT capability: Years 7, 8 and 9'**. The text links with **Sample Teaching Unit 8.2 for ICT** some aspects of which schools may have adopted within their Key Stage 3 scheme of work. Further information on how this text links with Sample Teaching Unit 8.2 can be downloaded from the teacher resources at www.payne-gallway.co.uk.

The book is designed to allow pupils to perform tasks independently within the context of a structured ICT lesson. Additional and extension tasks are included throughout the text to provide opportunities for progression to higher levels of achievement. Pupils will need access to computers with FrontPage Express and IrfanView. Both of these applications are available as free downloads. Download and installation instructions can be found in the resources section at www.payne-gallway.co.uk/FPExpress.

The pupil resources referred to throughout the text are freely available from the resources section at www.payne-gallway.co.uk/FPExpress.

Key Stage 3 ICT

Web Publishing with FrontPage Express

P Evans

Published by

PAYNE-GALLWAY
P U B L I S H E R S L T D

26-28 Northgate Street, Ipswich IP1 3DB
Tel: 01473 251097 • Fax: 01473 232758
www.payne-gallway.co.uk

A catalogue entry for this book is available from the British Library.

Copyright © P. Evans 2004

ISBN 1 904467 38 5

Published by Payne-Gallway Publishers Limited
26-28 Northgate Street, Ipswich IP1 3DB

Tel: +44 (0)1473 251097 • Fax: +44 (0)1473 232758 • E-mail: info@payne-gallway.co.uk

10 9 8 7 6 5 4 3 2 1

Cover Illustration © Richard Chasemore 2004

Design & Artwork by: direction123.com

Printed in Malta by: Gutenberg Press Limited

Chapter 1 Using HTML Code

In this chapter you will learn what HTML code is and use it to create a simple web page.

Viewing HTML code

To get started you need to load Internet Explorer. You probably know already that this is a web browser and we use it to view web pages.

▶ Either double-click the Internet Explorer icon on your desktop —————

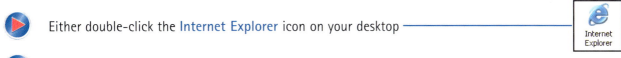

▶ or click Start at the bottom left of the screen, then click Programs, then click

▶ Click in the address bar and type www.payne-gallway.co.uk

This is the URL of the web site. URL stands for Uniform Resource Locator and describes the location of a web page or other file on the Internet.

▶ Press Enter.

You will see the home page of the web site for the publisher of this book.

Click View, Source on the main menu at the top of the screen.

This will open a window like the one shown below. This window contains the HTML code for this web page. HTML is short for hypertext mark-up language. The instructions in an HTML file tell a web browser like Internet Explorer about the content of a web page and how it should be displayed.

```
www.payne-gallway.co[1] - Notepad

File  Edit  Format  View  Help

<html>
<!-- DW6 -->
<head>
<title>welcome to Payne-Gallway</title>
<meta http-equiv="Content-Type" content="text/html; charset=iso-8859-1">
<META name="keywords" content="ECDL, ECDL4, ICDL, Pascal, Delphi, Logo, Co
<META name="description" content="The future in books. Payne-Gallway speci
<META name="revisit-after" content="60 days">
<META name="robots" content="all">
<META name="copyright" content="Payne-Gallway Publishers Limited">
<META name="publisher" content="Direction Advertising &amp; Design">
<META name="author" content="Direction Advertising &amp; Design">
<style type="text/css">
<!--
.topbarbg {  background-image:    url(graphics/orangetitle.jpg); backgroun
.title {  font-family: Arial, Helvetica, sans-serif; font-size: 18px; font
.bodycopy {  font-family: Arial, Helvetica, sans-serif; font-size: 12px; f
.footertext {  font-family: Arial, Helvetica, sans-serif; font-size: 10px;
.navigationlinks {  font-family: Arial, Helvetica, sans-serif; font-size:
-->
</style>
</head>
<body bgcolor="#FFFFFF" text="#000000" leftmargin="0" topmargin="0" margin

<!-- Word 2000, Word 2002, Excel, Access, Powerpoint, Publisher, Windows 2
<table width="615" border="0" cellspacing="0" cellpadding="0" height="76">
  <tr>
    <td width="249" valign="top" height="70" bgcolor="#F3A366"><a name="to
    <td width="108" valign="top" height="70" bgcolor="#F3A366"> <div align
    <td width="135" valign="top" height="70" bgcolor="#F3A366"> <table wid
        <form name="search" method=GET action=cgi-bin/search.pl>
          <input
type=hidden name="PerPage" value="5">
          <input type=hidden
name="Start" value="0">
        <tr>
          <td height="71"
width="135" bgcolor="#F3A366" valign="top" align="center"> <div align="lef
              <table width="135" border="0" cellspacing="0" cellpadding=
                <tr>
                  <td bgcolor="#F3A366"> </td>
                </tr>
```

You probably think this looks complicated but don't worry – it's divided up into special sections. Once you know what goes in each section it will be much easier to understand. The rest of this chapter explains this and shows you how to create a web page by writing HTML code.

Writing HTML code

To get started we need to load a text editing program. We will use this to create a file that contains the HTML code for our web page. The text editor we are going to use is called Notepad – follow the steps below to load this program.

 Click Start at the bottom left of the screen, then Programs, Accessories, Notepad.

If you can't load Notepad this way ask your teacher to help.

When Notepad has loaded you will see a window like the one below.

Now we're ready to start writing the HTML code for our web page.
HTML code contains special markers called **tags** enclosed in **<>** brackets.

Tags tell a web browser how to display the items on a web page. Tags normally come in pairs, at the beginning and end of the item they describe. The tag at the end of an item always has a **/** after the first **<** bracket.

Every HTML file has a start tag **<HTML>** at the beginning and an end tag **</HTML>** at the end. The other sections of the HTML code are placed between these tags.

Click in the Notepad window and enter the **<HTML>** and **</HTML>** tags on separate lines.

Your Notepad window should now look like the one below.

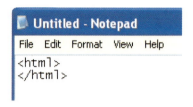

The HTML code in between the **<HTML>** and **</HTML>** tags is divided into two sections. The first of these is the **head section**. The contents of this section are contained inside the **<head>** and **</head>** tags. Information about the style and format of a page is placed in this section.

You'll normally find the pair of tags **<title>** and **</title>** in the head section. These tags contain a piece of text that is displayed in the top bar of a web browser's window to indicate the contents of the web page. The text in this section is also used by search engines to find the content of a page. The example below shows how the BBC uses this on its web site.

Next we'll add the head section along with a title to our HTML file.

Click next to the **<HTML>** tag in the Notepad window.

Press **Enter** to move onto the next line.

Enter the HTML code below.

```
<head>
<title>Popular search engines</title>
</head>
```

Your Notepad window should now look like the one below.

```
Untitled - Notepad
File  Edit  Format  View  Help
<html>
<head>
<title>Popular search engines</title>
</head>
</html>
```

The second section of an HTML file is the body section. The contents of this section are contained inside the <body> and </body> tags. Everything that will be displayed in the browser window when the web page is viewed is placed in this section. This includes all of the text, graphics, and links to other pages or web sites.

The next thing we'll do is add some tags to the body section to give us a heading on the page.

 Click next to the </head> tag in the Notepad window.

Press Enter to move onto the next line.

 Enter the HTML code below.

```
<body>
<h1>Some popular search engines</h1>
```

Notice that the tags <h1> and </h1> have been placed around the text to show it is a heading.

1 Creating hyperlinks

Now we're going to add some hyperlinks for popular search engines to the web page. These will be listed with the name of the search engine underneath the heading. When the web page is viewed in a web browser the name of the search engine will be underlined to show it is a hyperlink. The cursor arrow will also change to a hand shape when it is held over the hyperlink. Clicking on the hyperlink will take the user to the home page of the search engine.

Hyperlinks added in HTML use the **<a href>** and **</a>** tags. Text to describe the hyperlink is placed between these tags. In this case we're going to use the names of search engines. The URL for the web page or site is placed in quotation marks inside the **<a href>** tag after an equals (**=**) sign. An example of this is shown below.

This would display the text **Google** as a hyperlink. The user would be taken to the web site **www.google.com** when they clicked on the hyperlink.

Now put hyperlinks to four popular search engines onto the web page.

▶ Click next to the **</h1>** tag in the Notepad window.

▶ Press **Enter** to move onto the next line.

▶ Enter the HTML code below.

```
<a href="http://www.google.com">Google</a><br>
<a href="http://www.yahoo.com">Yahoo</a><br>
<a href="http://www.excite.com">Excite</a><br>
<a href="http://www.askjeeves.com">Ask Jeeves</a><br>
```

Notice that another new tag – the line break tag **
** – has been placed at the end of each line. This tag is used to start a new line – it needs no closing tag. If we didn't use this tag the names of the search engines would all appear next to each other on the same line.

The paragraph tag **<p>** can also be used to skip a line and start a new one. Although this needs no closing tag the **</p>** tag is sometimes used. This tag is also used to align text, so for example **<p align=right>** will line the text up on the right-hand side of the page. What do you think the tag to line text up in the middle of the page text might look like?

That's almost all the HTML code we need to create this web page. The last thing we need to do is close the body section.

 Click next to the last **
** tag in the Notepad window.

 Press **Enter** to move onto the next line and type **</body>**.

Your Notepad window should now look like the one below.

```
Untitled - Notepad
File  Edit  Format  View  Help
<html>
<head>
<title>Popular search engines</title>
</head>
<body>
<h1>Some popular search engines</h1>
<a href="http://www.google.com">Google</a><br>
<a href="http://www.yahoo.com">Yahoo</a><br>
<a href="http://www.excite.com">Excite</a><br>
<a href="http://www.askjeeves.com">Ask Jeeves</a><br>
</body>
</html>
```

Now we need to save this file.

 Click **File**, **Save** on the main menu at the top of the Notepad window.

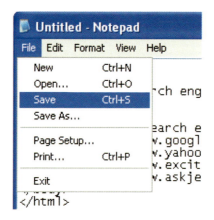

You should save this file to your network home directory or **My Documents** folder – ask your teacher if you're not sure how to do this.

 Type **page1.htm** in the **File name** box then click **Save**.

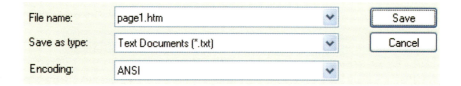

The **.htm** after the file name is very important. This identifies the file as HTML code and allows it to be viewed as a web page in a web browser.

Now we can see what this HTML code looks like as a web page.

 Open your network home directory or **My Documents** folder.

 You should see an icon like the one below labelled with the name **page1.htm**

page1.htm

 Double-click this icon.

Internet Explorer will load and display the web page - it should look like the one shown on the next page.

▶ Click on the hyperlinks and check they work – are you taken to the correct web site when you click on a link?

If your web page does not look like the one shown above or any of the hyperlinks don't work, there is probably a mistake in your HTML code. If this is the case follow the steps below to check it.

▶ Click View, Source on the main menu at the top of the screen.

The HTML code for the page will be displayed in a Notepad window.

▶ Compare this HTML code with the finished version shown on page 7.

▶ Correct any mistakes.

▶ Click File, Save on the main menu at the top of the screen.

▶ Close the Notepad window by clicking on the Close icon in the top right-hand corner. ———————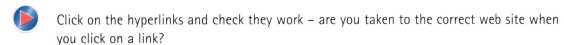

▶ Click View, Refresh on the main menu at the top of the Internet Explorer window.

Your page should now look like the one shown above. If it doesn't, repeat the steps above and check through your HTML code again. Ask your teacher to help if you still can't find any mistakes.

① Task A

You will need to view and edit the HTML code for your page to complete these tasks. Each time you make a change to the HTML code click **File**, **Save** in the Notepad window before clicking **View**, **Refresh** in the Internet Explorer window.

1. There are six levels of headings in HTML code, from **Heading 1** through to **Heading 6**. So far we have used the tags **<h1>** and **</h1>** for **Heading 1**. What do the other heading tags look like? Experiment with the heading tags in the HTML code for your page to find out.

2. Work out what the HTML tags for bold text are and add them to your HTML code so the page heading is displayed as bold text.

3. Work out what the HTML tags for italic text are and add them to your HTML code so the page heading is displayed as italic text.

When you've finished close Internet Explorer and Notepad by clicking the **Close** ———————— icon in the top right-hand corner of their windows.

Chapter 2 Web Site Design

Before any web site is created, the information it should contain and how different sections and pages will be linked together must be carefully planned. This will help to make sure the web site meets the needs of the target audience. In this chapter you will learn how to use diagrams to design web sites.

Before we get started make sure your teacher has given you a copy of Worksheet 2.

Web schemas

A web schema is a diagram that outlines the content of a series of web pages and shows the links between them. A web schema can describe a complete web site or a group of pages that forms one section of a web site. The web schema on the following page describes the main sections of a proposed web site for a pop group called Rainbow.

The schema shows the home page of the site at the centre. Linked to this page are three other main sections for merchandise, biographies and discography. Inside each section there is a set of web pages. If you look at the biography section you will see that there are four web pages – one for each member of the group and an index page.

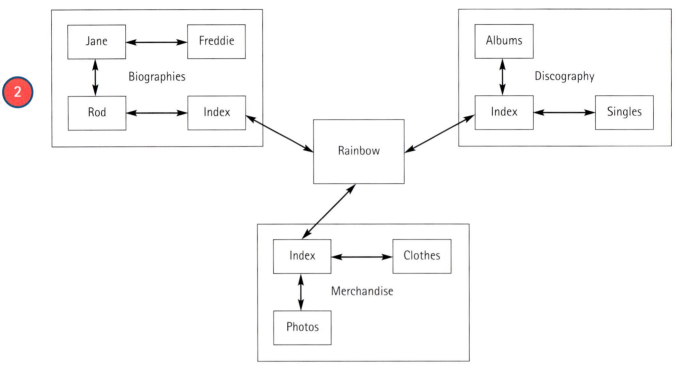

The text label on a section or page indicates what sort of information it is going to contain. So in the biography section, the page labelled Jane will contain information about this member of the band.

The hyperlinks between pages and sections are shown using arrows. Planning hyperlinks is an important part of designing web schema; we're going to look at this in more detail now.

Planning hyperlinks

A well-designed web site will have well-planned hyperlinks that allow users to navigate quickly and easily between different sections and pages. When you are drawing a web schema make sure you have included hyperlinks that will take users:

- from one page in a section to any other page in the same section;

- from one section to another section;

- easily back to the beginning of a section;

- easily back to the home page of the web site.

This advice for planning hyperlinks was not followed by the person who produced the web schema shown above. We're going to think about what these problems are by looking in more detail at the Biographies section of the web site.

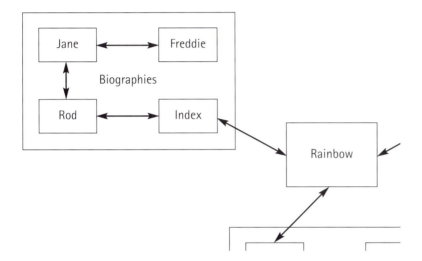

Look carefully at the links shown in this section of the schema. How would a user get from the Index to Freddie's page? There's no direct link between these pages so they couldn't go straight there. So what route would they have to take? Using the links shown, a user would need to move from the Index page to Rod's page, then on to Jane's page before finally moving to Freddie's page.

This is not an efficient way to navigate between these pages so the schema for this section of the web site must be improved. This could be done by changing the links so that users could move directly between the Index page and the other pages. If we did this the new schema would look like the one on the next page.

2

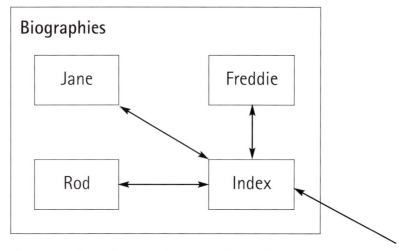

This section of the schema has been improved. It now shows that a user can move directly from the Index to any of the other three pages and back again. What other links would you need to add if you wanted to allow users the additional option of moving from one band member's page to another's without going back through the Index?

Task B

You will need your copy of Worksheet 2 to complete this task.

The web schema below describes the main sections of a proposed web site for Crossways High School. Only part of this schema has been completed.

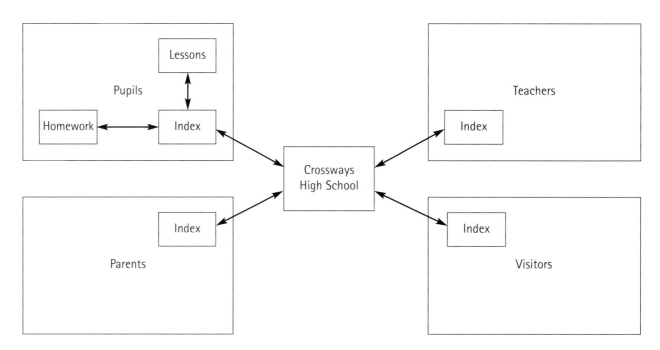

Only four sections of this web site are shown in the web schema. More sections will be needed before the web site designers can be sure it meets the needs of the target audience. One group of users who will form part of the target audience for this web site are pupils at the school. The type of information needed by these users is shown below. This example is also shown in the first row of the table on Worksheet 2.

Group of users	Information needed by this group of users
Pupils at the school	Lesson resources Homework resources

 Complete the second column on your copy of **Worksheet 2** to show the sort of information that might be needed by the different groups of users listed.

Task C

Your teacher will set you a task that will involve designing and producing some pages for one section of a much larger web site.

Draw a web schema for the section of the web site your teacher has allocated to you. As you prepare your schema remember to think about:

- what sort of information users of the web site will expect to see in your section;

- the hyperlinks that will be needed to allow users to navigate easily between the pages in your section;

- the hyperlinks that will be needed to allow users to navigate from your section to other sections of the web site;

- the hyperlinks that will be needed to allow users to navigate from your section back to the home page of the web site.

Chapter 3 Tables and Text

In this chapter you will begin learning how to use FrontPage Express to create web pages. You will start by creating a table and using it to help position text on a page.

Getting started

The first thing you need to do is create a folder to store all the files the web site will need. You should do this whenever you start work on a new web site.

 Open your network home directory or My Documents folder.

Ask your teacher what to do if you don't know which folder to use.

 Click File, New Folder.

 Type Crossways as the name for this folder.

Always choose a sensible name for the folder where the web site files will be stored. It is a good idea to use a name that has something to do with what the site is for or about. In this example we are creating some web pages for Crossways High School so we have called the folder Crossways.

The pupil resources for this book at www.payne-gallway.co.uk/FPExpress include a folder named Crossways.

 Copy the files from this Crossways folder to your own Crossways folder. Your teacher will tell you where to find these files and how to copy them.

When you've finished, your Crossways folder should contain all the files shown in the screenshot below.

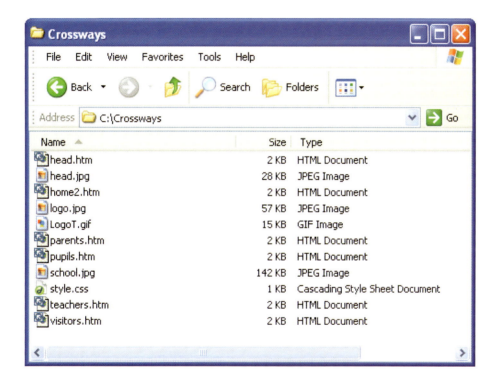

Now we are ready to load FrontPage Express. This can be done in one of two ways:

 Either double-click the FrontPage Express icon on your desktop ————————

 or click Start at the bottom left of the screen, then click Programs, then click

FrontPage Express will load – your screen should look like the one on the next page.

3

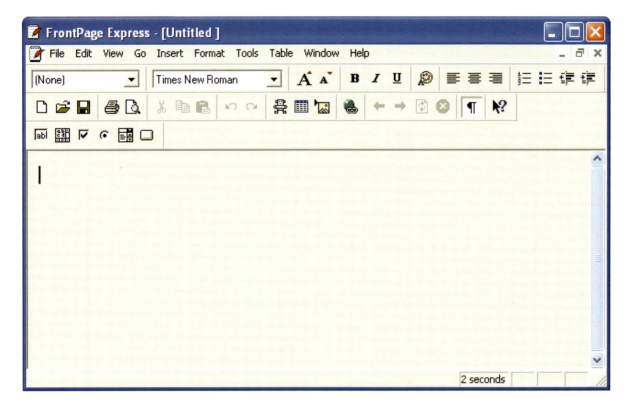

Now you can start setting up the home page of the web site.

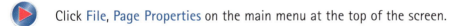

Click File, Page Properties on the main menu at the top of the screen.

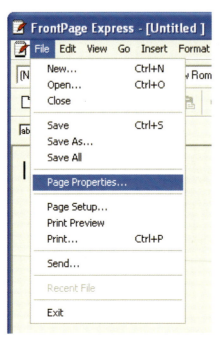

Click on the General tab if it isn't already selected.

 Click inside the Title box.

 Type Crossways High School Home Page and click OK.

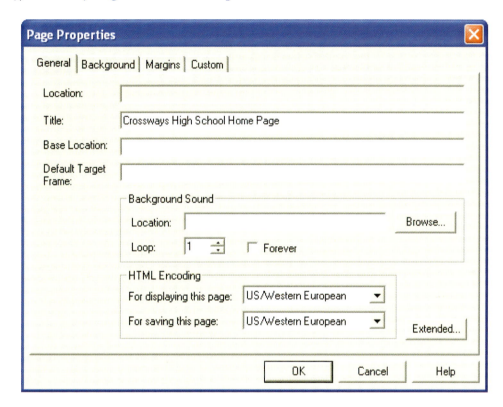

This is the text that will be displayed at the top of the browser window when this page is viewed with a web browser. All FrontPage has done is completed the **<title>...</title>** part of the HTML file for you. Follow the steps below to check this.

 Click View, HTML on the main menu at the top of the screen.

The HTML code for the page will be displayed in a window like the one shown below. You will see that the text 'Crossways High School Home Page' has been inserted between the **<title>...</title>** tags.

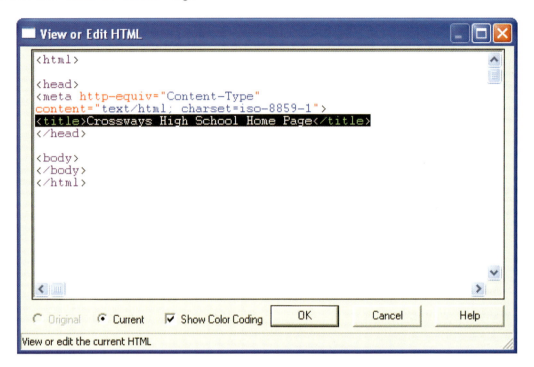

This is one advantage of using software like FrontPage Express to create web pages. The HTML code is generated automatically but you can still view and edit the instructions. Sometimes doing this is quicker and more efficient than trying to achieve the same results using the main FrontPage screen. We'll come back to this idea later on in the book.

 Click **OK** to return to the normal view of the page.

Designing page layouts

Ordinary HTML code can only be used to place objects on the left, right or centre of a page. Most web designers get around this problem by using tables for their page layout designs. This allows objects to be positioned by placing them inside individual cells in the table.

The page layout design for the Crossways High School home page is shown in the following diagram.

To build a page with this layout we will need to create a table with **three rows** and **three columns**. This will give us nine cells inside which we can place objects, the text and images indicated on the design.

All text in this cell centred;
Heading 1;
Arial font; colour black.

	Welcome to Crossways High school	School logo in this cell logo.jpg
Parents hyperlink to parents.htm **Pupils** hyperlink to pupils.htm **Teachers** hyperlink to teachers.htm **Visitors** hyperlink to visitors.htm	Picture of the school in this cell – school.jpg	**Message from the Headteacher** hyperlink to head.htm
	Headteacher; Mrs. B. Wheat B.Sc (Hons) e-mail: office@crossways.org.uk	

Text in this cell left-aligned; Heading 4; Arial font; colour black.

All text in this cell centred; Heading 5; Arial font; colour black.

Text in this cell centred; Heading 4 Arial font; colour black

When you produce designs for your own pages they will need to give information like this. You should also include comments explaining why you have chosen certain font styles, font sizes, headings and images. Don't try to produce your designs on a computer – it will be much quicker to use squared paper and draw them by hand. Another important point here is that you should always try to work out what size and shape of table you will need and show this clearly on your page design.

3 Creating a table

 Click Table, Insert Table... on the main menu at the top of the screen.

The Insert Table window will be displayed.

 Click in the Rows box.

Change the number of rows to 3.

 Click in the Columns box.

Change the number of columns to 3.

 Tick the Specify Width box.

Make sure the number next to it is 100 and in Percent is selected underneath. Choosing these options will make sure the table always fills the whole screen rather than adjusting itself to fit around the objects placed inside it.

The Insert Table window on your screen should now look exactly like the one shown on the next page.

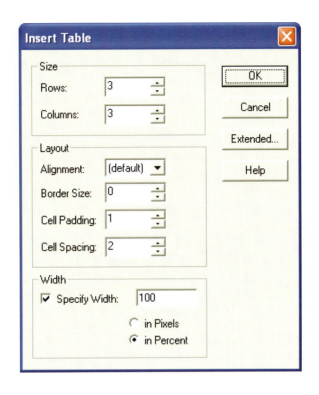

 Click OK.

A table bordered with a dotted outline will be displayed on your screen.

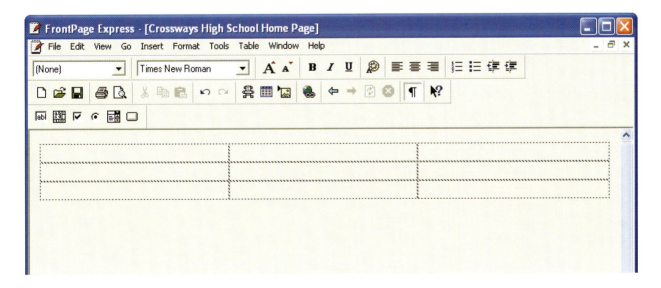

Adding text

Now we are ready to put some text on the page. We'll add the main heading for the page first.

▶ Click inside the middle cell of the first row in the table.

▶ Type Welcome to Crossways High School.

▶ Highlight the text.

▶ Click the Center button on the toolbar at the top of the screen to align the text in the centre of the cell.

▶ Click the arrow of the Change Font drop-down box at the top left side of the screen.

▶ Choose Arial in the list of fonts.

We have changed the font to Arial because this is a Sans Serif font. This type of font is often used on web sites because it looks much more modern than Serif fonts like Times New Roman.

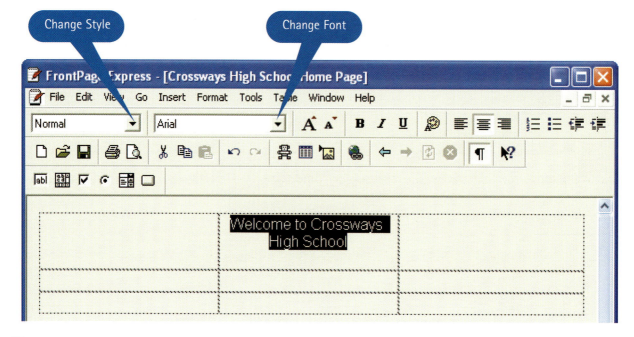

▶ Click the arrow of the Change Style drop-down box at the top left side of the screen.

Choose Heading 1 from the list.

You'll see there are six different heading styles numbered from 1 to 6. Heading 1 will give the largest size text. This is fine because we want this main heading to stand out on the page.

 Click just underneath the table to de-select the text and see how it looks – your page should look like the one below.

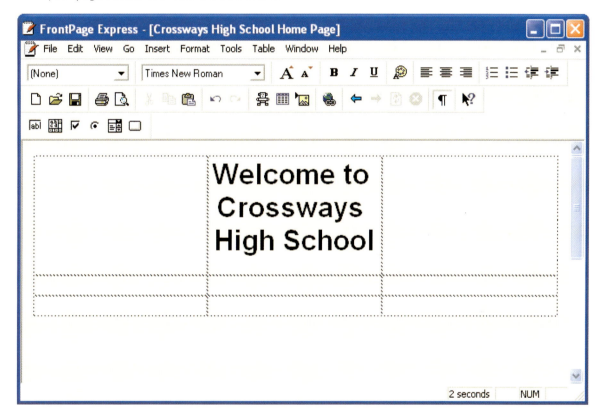

Next we'll add some text that will eventually become hyperlinks to other pages in the web site.

 Click inside the first cell of the second row in the table.

 Type the four lines of text shown below – press Enter after each line.

Parents
Pupils
Teachers
Visitors

 Highlight all of this text.

 Set the style to Heading 4.

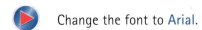 Change the font to Arial.

Add the text below to your page.

You should put this text in the second cell of the third row in the table:

Headteacher: Mrs. B. Wheat B.Sc. (Hons)
e-mail: enquiries@crossways.org.uk

Choose Heading 5 for this text, centre it and change the font to Arial.

Add the text below to your page.

You should put this text in the third cell of the second row in the table:

Message from the Headteacher

Choose Heading 4 for this text, centre it and change the font to Arial.

Your page should look like the one shown below.

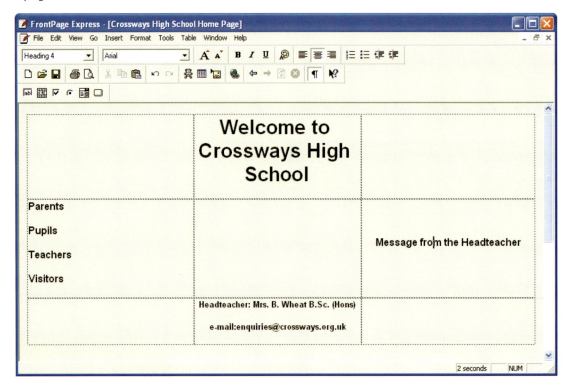

Saving and viewing your page

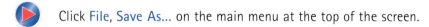 Click File, Save As... on the main menu at the top of the screen.

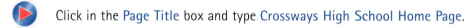 Click in the Page Title box and type Crossways High School Home Page.

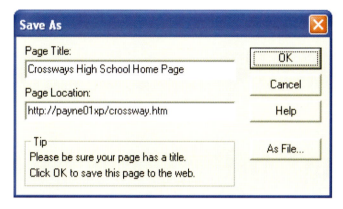

 Click As File...

Double-click the Crossways folder you created at the start of this chapter.

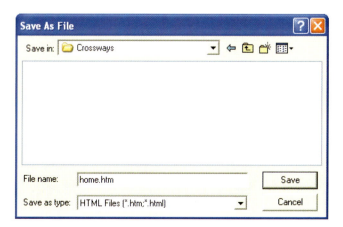 Click in the File name box and type home.htm

Click Save.

 Close FrontPage Express by clicking the Close icon in the top right-hand corner of the window.

Now we can see what this page looks like in a web browser.

 Open your network home directory or My Documents folder.

3

 Double-click the home.htm icon.

Internet Explorer will load and display the web page – it should look like the one shown below.

Welcome to
Crossways High
School

Parents

Pupils

Message from the Headteacher

Teachers

Visitors

Headteacher: Mrs. B. Wheat B.Sc. (Hons)

e-mail:enquiries@crossways.org.uk

 Close Internet Explorer by clicking the Close icon in the top right-hand corner ——————— of the browser window.

If you've completed this chapter and have some time to spare try the exercise that follows on the next few pages. This describes how to create and modify an ordinary table to match a particular page layout design. Being able to create tables of exactly the right size and shape is an important skill if you are going to start producing high-quality web pages.

Some more work with tables

 Load FrontPage Express.

We are going to create an ordinary table and modify it to match the outline page layout design shown below.

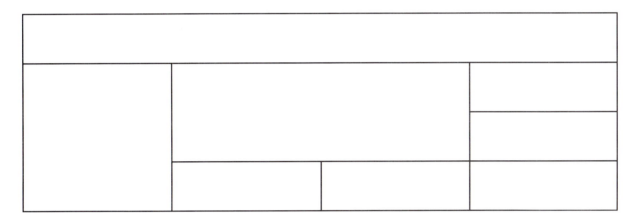

The first thing we need to do is create an ordinary table. We'll decide what size this table needs to be by counting the maximum number of rows and columns shown in the design above. If you do this you'll see there are four columns across and four rows down, so we need to start off with a table of this size.

 Click Table, Insert Table... on the main menu at the top of the screen.

The Insert Table window will be displayed.

 Click in the Rows box.

Change the number of rows to 4.

 Click in the Columns box.

Change the number of columns to 4.

 Tick the Specify Width box.

Make sure the number next to it is 100 and in Percent is selected underneath.

Click **OK**.

The table will be displayed on your screen.

Now the standard table has been created we can customise it by merging cells together to get a shape that matches the page layout design.

 The first thing we'll do is merge the cells in the first row of the table to form a single cell across the top of the table.

 Click in the first cell in the top left-hand corner of the table.

Click on **Table, Select Row** on the main menu at the top of the screen.

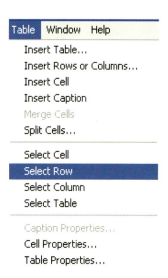

The first row of the table will be highlighted.

 Click **Table, Merge Cells** on the main menu at the top of the screen.

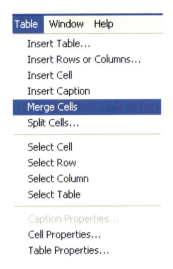

The cells in the first row of the table will be merged to form a single cell across the top of the table.

Next we'll merge the remaining cells in the first column of the table to form a single cell on the left side of the table.

 Click inside the first cell of the second row.

 Click Table, Select Cell on the main menu at the top of the screen.

The cell will be highlighted.

 3 ▶ Hold the Shift key down and click in each of the two cells underneath.

▶ Let go of the Shift key.

The three cells in the first column will be highlighted.

▶ Click Table, Merge Cells on the main menu at the top of the screen.

Your table should now look like this:

The last thing we need to do is merge four cells in the middle of the table to form a single cell.

Click inside the second cell of the second row.

click here

 Click Table, Select Cell on the main menu at the top of the screen.

 Hold the Shift key down.

 Click inside the next cell in this row and the two cells underneath.

 Let go of the Shift key.

The four cells in the middle of the table should be highlighted.

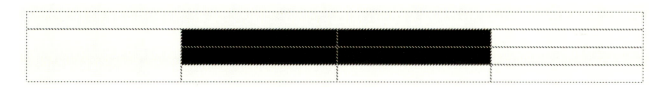

 Click Table, Merge Cells on the main menu at the top of the screen.

The four highlighted cells will be merged to form a single large cell in the middle of the table. The layout of your table should now match the page layout shown on page 29.

Once a standard table has been modified to match a page layout design, the web page can be built by inserting and positioning images and text in the cells. The task below gives you two more page layout designs to produce tables for.

Task D

▶ To get started, click on the New File icon on the toolbar at the top of the ───────── 🗋
FrontPage Express window.

▶ Click No if you are asked about saving changes.

3 Create and modify tables to match the outline page layout designs shown below.

Page layout design 1

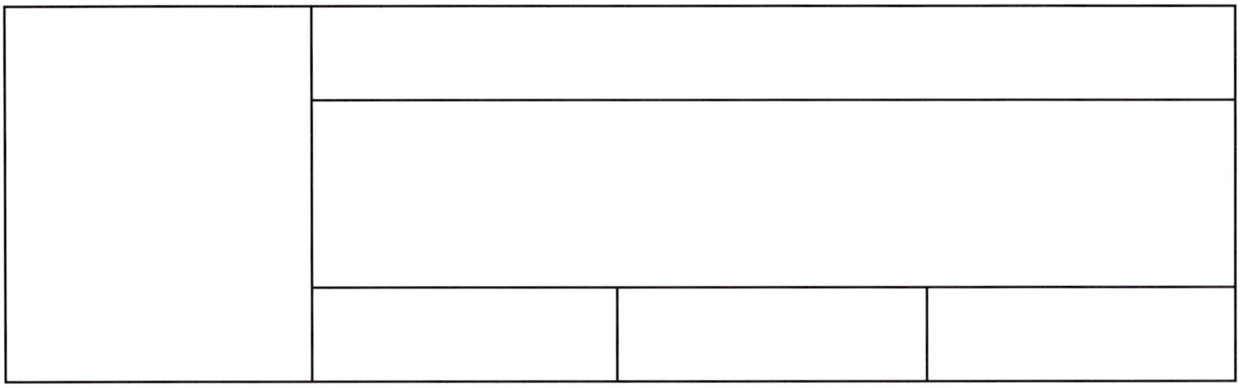

Page layout design 2

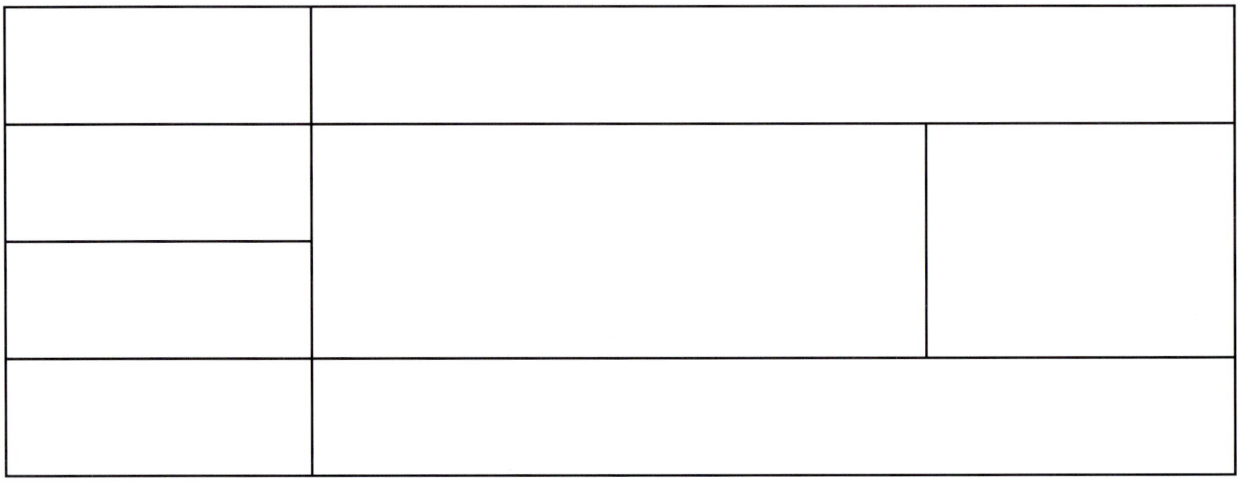

▶ When you've finished, close FrontPage Express.

Chapter 4 Hyperlinks and Images

In this chapter you will learn how to use FrontPage Express to create hyperlinks and add images to pages. You will also learn how to work with images to make web pages more suitable for a wide range of users.

Getting started

To get started you need to load FrontPage Express and open the home page you saved at the end of the last chapter. If you didn't complete the last chapter ask your teacher to show you where to find a finished version of the file.

Load FrontPage Express.

Click File, Open... on the main menu at the top of the screen.

Click Browse... and find your network home directory or My Documents folder.

Double-click the Crossways folder to open it.

The home.htm page you saved at the end of the last chapter should be listed.

Click home.htm and Open.

Your Crossways High School home page will open.

Creating hyperlinks

Next we'll use some of the text in the table to create hyperlinks to other pages in the web site. Some of the pages have already been created and stored in the **Crossways** folder (see the .htm files).

 Double-click the **Parents** heading to highlight it.

 Click **Insert**, **Hyperlink...** on the main menu at the top of the screen.

You can also click the **Insert Hyperlink** button on the toolbar to insert or edit a hyperlink. ———

The **Create Hyperlink** window will be displayed.

 Click in the **URL:** box.

 Type **parents.htm** – this is the name of the web page we want to be displayed when a user clicks this hyperlink.

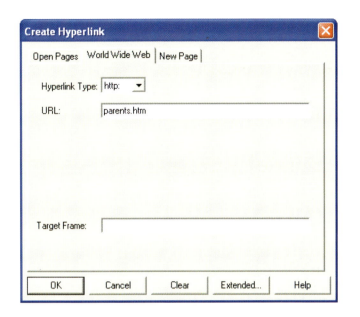

 Click **OK**.

 Now create hyperlinks for the other choices listed in this cell. You must remember to give each page the same name as the text you've highlighted and add **.htm** to the end.

Once you've done this, the only other hyperlink is on the right of the page to link to a message from the Headteacher.

 Highlight the **Message from the Headteacher** tex.

 Create a hyperlink to link this text to the web page called **head.htm**.

When you've finished your page should look like the one below.

	Welcome to Crossways High School	
Parents Pupils Teachers Visitors		Message from the Headteacher
	Headteacher: Mrs. B. Wheat B.Sc. (Hons) e-mail:enquiries@crossways.org.uk	

Now you are ready to save the page before viewing it in Internet Explorer.

 Click **File**, **Save** on the main menu at the top of the screen.

 View the web page in **Internet Explorer**.

 Try clicking on each of the hyperlinks.

Most of them should lead to pages that are 'under construction'. Only the 'Message from the Headteacher' hyperlink will lead to a finished web page. Notice every page has a hyperlink that leads back to the home page.

  When you've finished, close Internet Explorer by clicking on the **Close** icon in the top ——————— right-hand corner of the browser window.

You probably think most of these pages aren't very interesting or useful at the moment. How could they be improved? Your first suggestion might be to add some images to the pages – we'll look at how to do this next.

Inserting images

Before we add any images to this web page look at the bottom right-hand corner of the FrontPage window. Had you noticed it said **2 seconds**? This is the estimated time the page would take to download over a slow 28.8K dial-up Internet connection. We'll see how this changes as we add images to the page.

 Click inside the last cell of the first row in the table.

 Click **Insert** and **Image...** on the main menu at the top of the screen.

The Image window will be displayed.

 Click Browse.

 Make sure you're still inside the Crossways folder in your network home directory or My Documents folder – ask your teacher to help if you can't find this.

 Click on the file called logo.jpg and Open.

You'll notice a problem straight away – this image is far too big! You need to make it a lot smaller. There are two ways this can be done. You could resize the image by clicking on it and using the black marquee squares in the corners just as if it were a piece of clipart in a word-processed document.

You could also specify an exact size in pixels for the image – this is the method we're going to use in this example because as you develop more of your own web pages this is something that you might need to do. We're going to specify a size of 100 wide by 100 high for the school logo.

Before we do this look at the estimated download time at the bottom of the screen: you'll see it has changed to 30 seconds. This means that even with the page unfinished it would take someone with a slow Internet connection around half a minute to load it. This is something you'll need to consider carefully as you add images to your web pages. Research shows users don't like to wait a long time for pages on web sites to load – you've probably experienced this yourself and moved quickly onto a different site.

Now let's carry on and make the logo smaller – do you think this will improve the download time?

 Click on the school logo with the right mouse button.

 Choose Image Properties... from the menu that appears next to the logo.

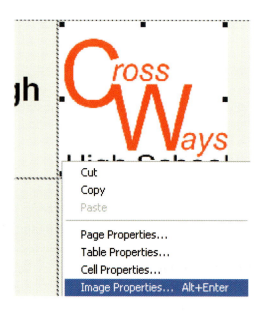

The Image Properties window will be displayed.

 Click on the Appearance tab and tick the Specify Size box.

 Make sure in Pixels is selected underneath both the Width and Height boxes.

Change the numbers in the Width and Height boxes to 100.

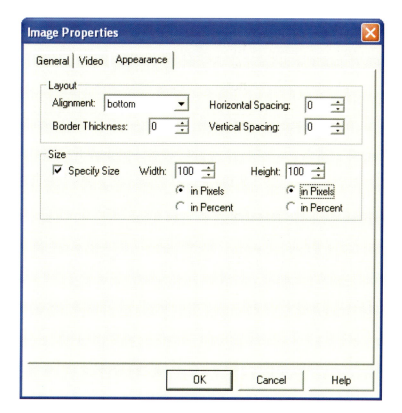

 Click OK. The resized school logo will be displayed on the page.

 Click the Center button on the toolbar at the top of the screen to align the logo ————— ≡ in the centre of the cell.

Look again at the estimated download time at the bottom of the screen – you will see it is still 30 seconds. You might have thought that changing the size of the image would improve this. The reason it hasn't changed is because all we've done is changed the size the image should be displayed at. We haven't done anything to change the size of the logo.jpg file itself. This file needs to be downloaded before it can be displayed, whenever users are trying to look at this web page on the Internet. Later in this chapter we'll look at how download times can be improved by reducing the size of image files.

Task E

1. Place an image of the school in the centre of the web page.
   Use the Insert Image command on the main menu to place the image school.jpg in the centre of the page – this file is inside the Crossways folder in your network home directory or My Documents folder.

2. The image will be too large when it is inserted. Choose Edit and Image Properties on the main menu and use the Appearance tab to reduce the image size to 550 pixels wide by 250 pixels high.

3. Save the page.

Once you've completed this task your page should look something like the one below. Look again at the estimated download time at the bottom of the screen and you will see it has gone up to 106 seconds. This means that even with the page unfinished it would take more than a minute and a half to load over a slow Internet connection. This is something we must improve. We'll look at how to do this by working with the image files using a simple graphics package.

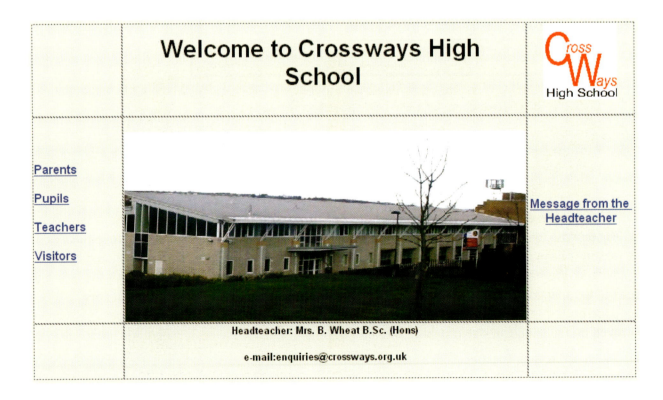

Working with images

The software we are going to use to work with our image files is called IrfanView – this is a simple image-viewing and editing program. There are lots of other more sophisticated image-editing programs available such as MS Photo Editor and Paint Shop Pro, some of which you might have on your own computer or those in school. Don't be afraid to try these programs out as well.

The first thing we need to do is load IrfanView.

 Either double-click the IrfanView icon on your desktop.—————————————

 or click Start at the bottom left of the screen, then click Programs, then click

IrfanView will load – you'll see a window like this:

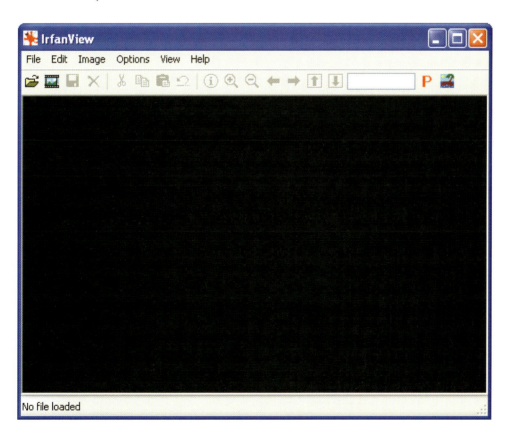

 Click File, Open on the main menu at the top of the IrfanView window.

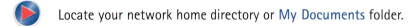 Locate your network home directory or **My Documents** folder.

 Double-click on the **Crossways** folder to open it.

 Click **once** on the **logo.jpg** file.

Some information about this file will be displayed.

4

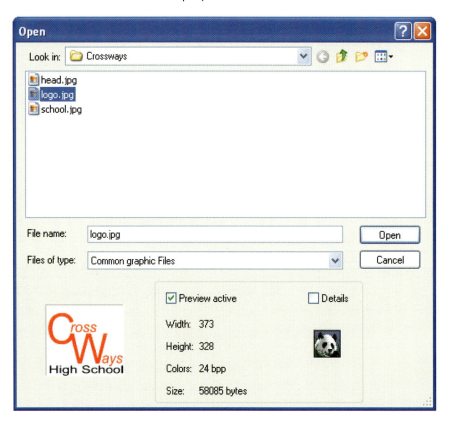

Look at the bottom of this window. You will see that the current size of this file is **58085 bytes** – this is the figure we need to reduce in order to make the web page load more quickly.

The technique we'll use for this image is to save it as a different file type. Image files come in many different types; you probably already know that two of the main types are **JPEG** and **GIF**. JPEG images can contain 16 million colours and are best for photographs. GIF images can only contain 256 colours and are better for drawings and simple designs. At the moment the school logo is a JPEG file. This is a simple image and only has a few colours so it would be better stored as a GIF file. Two useful features of GIF images are that they can be animated or have transparent backgrounds. The steps below describe how to convert the school logo from a JPEG to a GIF.

 Click **Open** to load the school logo image into IrfanView.

Click File, Save As on the main menu at the top of the IrfanView window.

 Click the down-arrow next to the Save as type box. A list of file types will be displayed.

 Click on GIF – Compuserve GIF in the list.

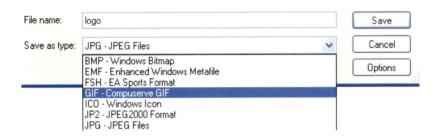

 Click the Options button.

A set of JPEG/GIF save options will be displayed.

 Tick Save Interlaced in the GIF section.

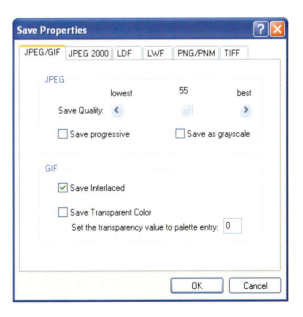

 Click OK and then click Save.

Choosing the Save Interlaced option here will help users with a slow Internet connection. The detail in an interlaced GIF image will start off fuzzy and appear to fade in until the image is complete. This makes the image appear to take less time to load.

Another advantage is that the user can sometimes get enough information about the image as it loads to decide if they need to wait before moving on.

Let's see what effect the change of file type has had on the size of the file.

 Click File, Open on the main menu at the top of the IrfanView window.

 Make sure you are still looking inside the Crossways folder in your network home directory or My Documents folder.

 Click once on the logo.gif file.

4 The information about this file will be displayed.

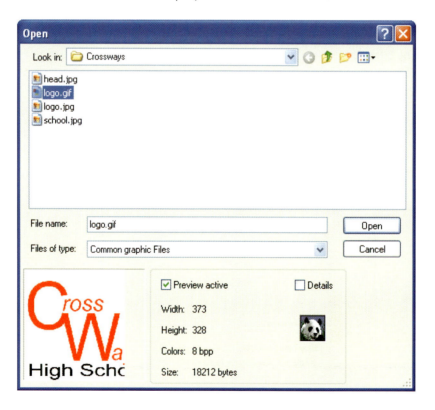

You'll see the size of the file has gone down – it's more than three times smaller than the original JPEG file!

Next we'll try to reduce the file size of the school photograph. Since this image is a photograph already stored as a JPEG there's no point in changing the file type. What we can do is compress the JPEG file. The following steps describe how to do this.

Click File, Open on the main menu at the top of the IrfanView window.

 Make sure you are still looking inside the Crossways folder in your network home directory or My Documents folder.

 Click once on the school.jpg file.

The information about this file will be displayed.

You'll see the current size of the file is 144864 bytes.

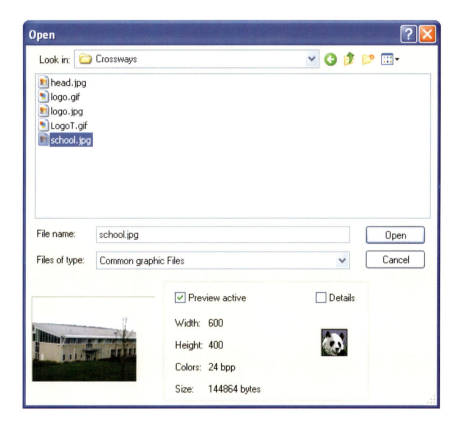

4

 Click Open to load the school logo image into IrfanView.

 Click File, Save As on the main menu at the top of the IrfanView window.

 Click the down-arrow next to the Save as type box

A list of file types will be displayed.

 Click on JPG – JPEG Files in the list.

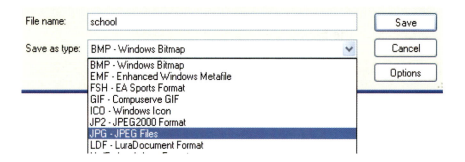

 Click the Options button.

The JPEG/GIF save options will be displayed.

 Move the Save Quality slider in the JPEG section to 55.

 Click OK and then click Save.

 Click Yes to replace the existing file.

Let's see what effect compressing the file has had on its size.

 Click File, Open on the main menu at the top of the IrfanView window.

Make sure you are still looking inside the Crossways folder in your network home directory or My Documents folder.

 Click once on the school.jpg file.

The updated information about the file will be displayed.

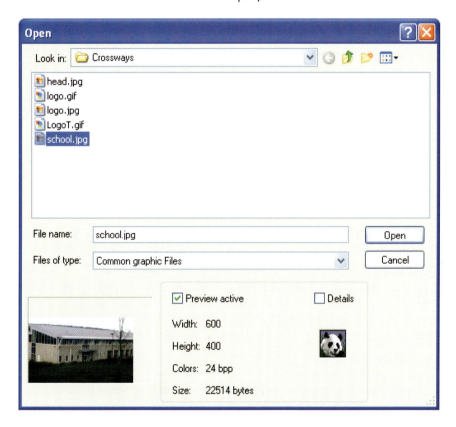

You'll see the size of this file has gone down from about 144Kb to 22Kb – quite an impressive reduction! We could try compressing this file more but eventually the quality of the displayed image will become poor. If you have time, experiment further with this using lower compression to see how low you can go before noticing any change in the image.

 Close IrfanView.

Now we can load FrontPage Express and see if the estimated download time of the page has gone down.

 Load FrontPage Express.

 Click File, Open on the main menu at the top of the screen.

Click Browse and find your network home directory or My Documents folder.

 Double-click on the Crossways folder to open it.

 Click home.htm and Open.

You should see a page like the one below with an estimated download time of 42 seconds.

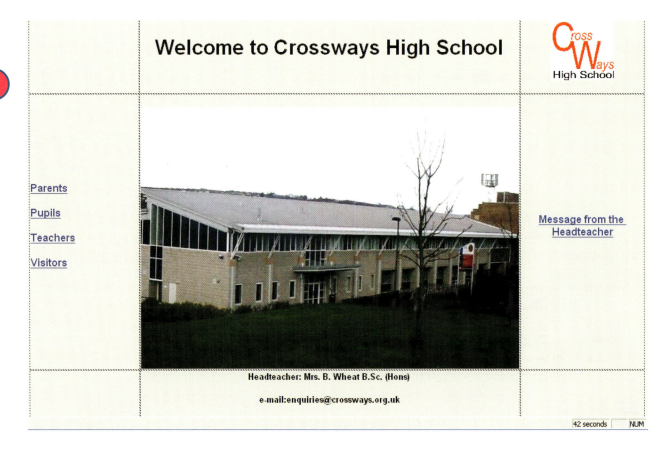

You might think this was a lot of effort for not much improvement in download time but there's one thing we still need to do.

 Click View, HTML on the main menu at the top of the screen.

The HTML code for the page will be displayed.

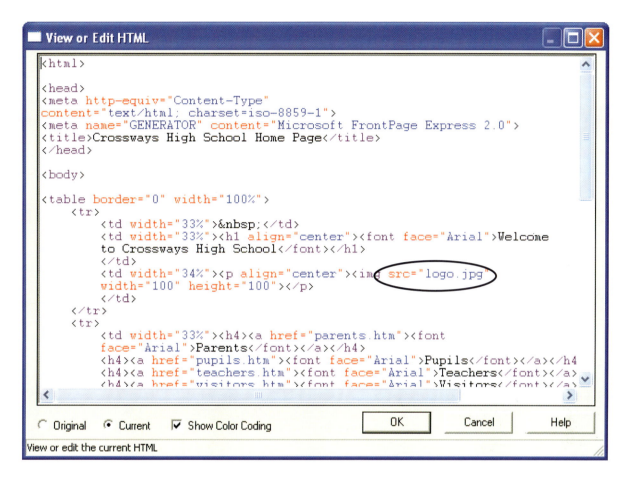

```
<html>

<head>
<meta http-equiv="Content-Type"
content="text/html; charset=iso-8859-1">
<meta name="GENERATOR" content="Microsoft FrontPage Express 2.0">
<title>Crossways High School Home Page</title>
</head>

<body>

<table border="0" width="100%">
    <tr>
        <td width="33%"> </td>
        <td width="33%"><h1 align="center"><font face="Arial">Welcome
        to Crossways High School</font></h1>
        </td>
        <td width="34%"><p align="center"><img src="logo.jpg"
        width="100" height="100"></p>
        </td>
    </tr>
    <tr>
        <td width="33%"><h4><a href="parents.htm"><font
        face="Arial">Parents</font></a></h4>
        <h4><a href="pupils.htm"><font face="Arial">Pupils</font></a></h4
        <h4><a href="teachers.htm"><font face="Arial">Teachers</font></a>
        <h4><a href="visitors.htm"><font face="Arial">Visitors</font></a>
```

View or Edit HTML — Original / Current / Show Color Coding — OK — Cancel — Help

View or edit the current HTML

Look carefully at the section of the HTML that describes the school logo. You should notice that it is referring to the JPEG version of the file logo.jpg. We need to change this to refer to the GIF version of the file. The quickest way is to just change the HTML rather than deleting the image and inserting it again on the main FrontPage screen.

 Click on the line of HTML code circled in the example above and change the file name from logo.jpg to logo.gif.

 Click OK.

The page looks exactly the same but the estimated download time has gone down to around 20 seconds – this is considerably better than 106 seconds!

 Save the web page and close FrontPage Express.

 Load this web page in Internet Explorer and see how it looks.

Task F

1. Design the page layout for the first page of the web site section your teacher has allocated to you. As you prepare your design think about:

   - what information users will expect to see on the page;

   - the text and images you will need to include;

   - whether the page will need a menu with a list of links to other pages – what will be the best position for this?

   - whether links to other web sites need to be included;

   - what size table you will need to position items on the page – how many rows and columns will it need and will cells need merging to get the right shape?

2. Use FrontPage Express to create the web page shown on your design: follow the steps below to do this.

   - Create a new folder in your network home directory or My Documents folder – this is where the files for your web site will be stored. Use a name that has something to do with what your web site is about.

   - Prepare the images you need and make sure they are saved in a folder you have created for the web site.

   - Load FrontPage Express and create a table – check your design to see how many rows and columns you need.

   - Add text and create hyperlinks.

   - Collect, prepare and insert images.

Chapter 5 Using Colour

In this chapter you will learn how to use colour to change the appearance of web pages in FrontPage Express. Using colour effectively can improve the appearance of web pages. It is also a good way to develop a corporate image for a web site. If a company or organisation always uses the same colour scheme in things like its logo, letter heads and advertising then users of the company's web site will expect to see the same sort of style on its web pages.

Getting started

 Load FrontPage Express.

To get started you need to load the sample web page called home2.htm from the Crossways directory inside your network home directory or My Documents folder.

 Click File, Open... on the main menu at the top of the screen.

 Click Browse and find your network home directory or My Documents folder.

 Double-click on the Crossways folder to open it.

 Click home2.htm and Open.

5

You should see a page like this:

This is a redesigned version of the Crossways High School home page. The Headteacher wasn't very happy with the original version and suggested some changes. She was much happier with this version but felt it lacked a corporate image. The web designer suggested that using the school colours of red and silver on the page might help. The new colour scheme was agreed and the page was changed again. The latest version of the page is shown below.

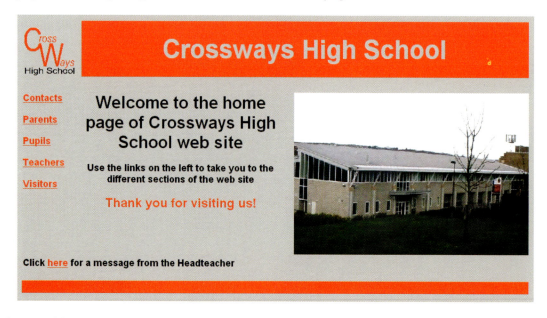

What do you think of this version of the page? Does it look better? Was the web designer right about using the school colours? Would this page appeal to a wide range of users? Would there be any users who might find it difficult to view the page now?

The rest of this chapter describes how the web designer added colour to the web page. You probably have different ideas about how colour could have been used more effectively on this page. Once you know how to work with colour in FrontPage Express you can try changing the page again and seeing if your version is better.

Page background colour

We are going to start by changing the background colour of the page to silver and the colour of the hyperlinks to red.

 Click Format, Background on the main menu at the top of the screen.

The Page Properties window will be displayed.

 Click the down-arrow next to the Background box. A list of colours will be displayed.

 Click on Silver.

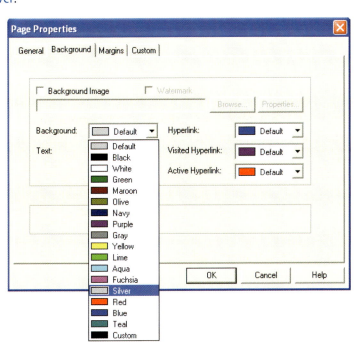

Click the down-arrow next to the Hyperlink box.

 Click on Red in the list of colours.

 Click OK.

The page background will change to silver and the hyperlink colour to red.

Cell colour

FrontPage Express allows you to change the colour of individual cells and groups of cells in a table. To get the page looking like the one shown on Page 54 we will need to change the colour of cells at the top and bottom of the page. We'll start by changing the colour of the cell at the top of the page containing the main heading.

 Click in the third cell of the first row in the table where the main page heading Crossways High School is displayed.

 Click Table, Select Cell on the main menu at the top of the screen.

Click Table, Cell Properties on the main menu.

The Cell Properties window will be displayed.

Click the down-arrow next to the Background box.

A list of colours will be displayed.

Click on Red.

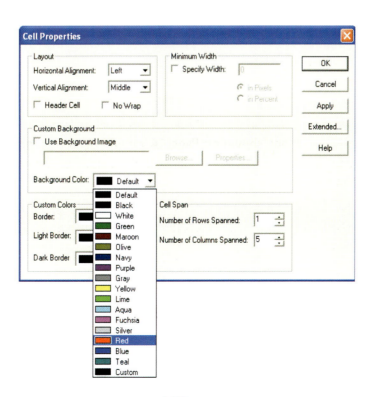

Click OK.

The colour of this cell will change to red.

The first row of the table should now look like this:

Now we need to change the font colour of the text in this cell to silver.

 Highlight the text in this cell.

  Click Format, Font on the main menu at the top of the screen.

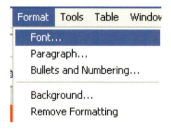

The Page Properties window will be displayed.

 Click the down-arrow next to the Background box.

A list of colours will be displayed.

 Click on Silver.

The first row of the table should now look like this.

Next we need change the cell colour of the last row in the table to red so that it looks like the one on the next page.

Click here for a message from the Headteacher

▶ Click in the bottom row of the table.

▶ Click Table, Select Cell on the main menu at the top of the screen.

▶ Click Table, Cell Properties on the main menu at the top of the screen.

▶ Change the background colour of this cell to silver.

▶ Now change the font colour of the message, "Thank you for visiting us!" to red. When you've finished, this part of the page should look like the one below.

Use the links on the left to take you to the different sections of the web site

Thank you for visiting us!

Those are all the changes the web designer made to the page.

▶ Save the web page and close FrontPage Express.

Now we can see what the finished web page looks like in a web browser.

▶ Open the Crossways folder in your network home directory or My Documents folder.

▶ Double-click the home2.htm icon.

Internet Explorer will load and display the new version of the page – it should look like the one shown at the beginning of this chapter.

▶ When you've finished close Internet Explorer by clicking on the Close icon in the top ——— ☒ right-hand corner the browser window.

Chapter 6 Using Style Sheets

In this chapter you will learn how to use style sheets. A style sheet is a set of instructions that defines how a web page should look. Style sheet instructions are stored in a separate file from the HTML code for a page. Style sheets are linked to web pages using a special HTML command. Using style sheets offers the advantage of being able to change the appearance of a complete web site or group of pages by editing just one set of instructions. Using style sheets is a good way to show you can work efficiently when creating or changing web pages in order to take into account the needs of different users.

Using style sheets

To get started you need to load the sample web page called head.htm from the Crossways folder inside your network home directory or My Documents folder.

 When your web browser has loaded and opened the **head.htm** file, you should see this web page:

5

Crossways High School

Message from the Headteacher

Thank you for taking some time to visit Crossways High School web site. I hope the information and resources presented here will help you to find out more about our school and the excellent standard of education we are proud to provide.

We believe in setting the highest standards in all areas of school life, centred on work, behaviour and attendance. Crossways is a school where all pupils are treated as individuals and encouraged to realise their full potential.

We have very high expectations of behaviour. Our aim is to create a caring and productive atmosphere where pupils feel safe and happy. Pupils' respect for each other and their excellent working relationships with staff make Crossways a school where everyone can succeed.

I am very proud to be the Headteacher of Crossways and look forward to working for the continued success of our school.

Barbara Wheat, B.Sc (Hons)

Headteacher

Home

You are going to use a set of instructions stored in a style sheet file called **style.css** to change the appearance of this web page.

 Click View, Source on the main menu at the top of your web browser window to display the HTML code for this page.

To make a web browser use style sheet instructions, a link to the style sheet file must be put in the head section of the HTML code for the page. The steps below describe how to do this.

 Click next to the </title> tag in the head section and press Enter to start a new line.

 Enter the HTML command shown below.

<link rel="stylesheet" href="style.css">

The HTML code at the bottom of the **<head>** section should now look like this:

```
<title>Crossways High School</title>
<link rel="stylesheet" href="style.css">
</head>
```

The style sheet file **style.css** contains the instructions shown below.

```
BODY   {font-family: Antigoni; color: black; font-size: 10pt; background-color: white}
TD     {font-family: Antigoni; color: black; font-size: 10pt; background-color: white}

H1     {font-size: 24pt}
H2     {font-size: 18pt}
H3     {font-size: 14pt}
H4     {font-size: 12pt}

A:hover {color: blue; background-color: white; text-decoration: none}
A:link {color: red; background-color: white}
A:visited {color: black; background-color: white; text-decoration: none}
```

6

What changes might you see once these style sheet instructions have been applied to this web page? Spend a couple of minutes looking at the instructions and thinking about this question.

Now let's see if you were right. We'll do this by saving the changes to the HTML code and refreshing the view of the page in your web browser.

 Click File, Save on the main menu at the top of the Notepad window.

 Close Notepad by clicking the Close icon in the top right-hand corner of the window.

Now apply the changes described in the style sheet by refreshing the view of the web page in your browser window.

 Click View, Refresh on the main menu at the top of your web browser window.

You can also do this by clicking the Refresh button on the toolbar at the top of the screen.
Refresh

The view of the web page will be refreshed. Were you right about how the style sheet instructions would change the appearance of the page? It should look like the screenshot below, but you may find your page looks just as it did before. This is probably because your computer does not have the Antigoni font installed. If this is the case, you need to edit the style sheet.

Crossways High School

CrossWays High School

Message from the Headteacher

Thank you for taking some time to visit Crossways High School web site. I hope the information and resources presented here will help you to find out more about our school and the excellent standard of education we are proud to provide.

We believe in setting the highest standards in all areas of school life, centred on work, behaviour and attendance. Crossways is a school where all pupils are treated as individuals and encouraged to realise their full potential.

We have very high expectations of behaviour. Our aim is to create a caring and productive atmosphere where pupils feel safe and happy. Pupils' respect for each other and their excellent working relationships with staff make Crossways a school where everyone can succeed.

I am very proud to be the Headteacher of Crossways and look forward to working for the continued success of our school.

Barbara Wheat, B.Sc (Hons)

Headteacher

Home

Editing style sheets

Style sheets can be created and edited using a text-editing program like Notepad. You are going to edit the style sheet from the last example to change the appearance of the web page again.

The first two lines of instructions in this style sheet are shown below. These instructions describe the fonts that the web page should use. In this example the font style is Antigoni light, the font colour is black and the font size is 10 points.

BODY {font-family: Antigoni; color: black; font-size: 10pt; background-color: white}
TD   {font-family: Antigoni; color: black; font-size: 10pt; background-color: white}

When you are choosing fonts for a web page you should remember that not every user who views the page will have the same fonts on their computer as you have on yours. The font specified here is Antigoni which is not one of the most common fonts. If you use fonts that some users don't have on their computers they won't be able to view your pages properly. This problem can be avoided by using a style sheet and listing a choice of more common fonts like Arial and Tahoma. We'll try this now by using Notepad to edit the instructions in the style.css file.

6

 Load Notepad.

 Click File, Open on the main menu at the top of the Notepad window.

 Locate your network home directory or My Documents folder.

 Double-click the Crossways folder to open it.

 Make sure the Files of type box is displaying All Files.

 Click on style.css and Open.

The instructions for this style sheet will be displayed in the Notepad window.

```
style.css - Notepad

File   Edit   Format   View   Help

BODY       {font-family: Antigoni;  color: black;  font-size
TD         {font-family: Antigoni;  color: black;  font-size


H1         {font-size: 24pt}
H2         {font-size: 18pt}
H3         {font-size: 14pt}
H4         {font-size: 12pt}
```

 Change the first two lines of these instructions so they are the same as those shown below.

BODY {font-family: Tahoma; Arial; sans-serif; color: black; font-size: 10pt; background-color: white}
TD   {font-family: Tahoma; Arial; sans-serif; color: black; font-size: 10pt; background-color: white}

We have replaced the Antigoni font with Tahoma which is very common and found on most computers. By making these changes you are also making sure that if another user's computer didn't have the Tahoma font, their web browser would look for Arial instead. If Arial wasn't on their computer, their web browser would use any other available sans serif font.

 Click File, Save on the main menu at the top of the Notepad window.

 Now apply the changes described in the style sheet by refreshing the view of the web page in your browser window.

Task G

Experiment with the style sheet by making changes to the first two lines:

BODY {font-family: Tahoma; Arial; sans-serif; color: black; font-size: 10pt; background-color: white}
TD   {font-family: Tahoma; Arial; sans-serif; color: black; font-size: 10pt; background-color: white}

You could make changes like these:

▶ Change the font Tahoma in the first line to Comic Sans.

▶ Change the font colour in the first line to red.

▶ Change the font size in the first line to 14pt.

Each time you make a change to the style sheet save it and refresh the web page in the browser window.

When you've finished, close Notepad and Internet Explorer by clicking on the Close ———— 6
icon in the top right-hand corner of their windows.

Some useful web sites

If you want to find out more about good web design try visiting some of these web sites:

www.thetipsbank.com/webdesign.htm for web design tips.

http://webreference.com/greatsite.html for advice on "What makes a great web site".

If you want to find out more about HTML try visiting this web site:

www.w3.org/MarkUp/Guide/

If you want to build web pages by writing your own HTML code, AceHTML is a useful program. This allows you to build HTML files by choosing from a full list of commands. Download AceHTML from

http://freeware.acehtml.com

To find out more about style sheets try visiting some of these web sites:

www.w3.org/MarkUp/Guide/Style

www.htmlhelp.com/reference/css/quick-tutorial.html

www.pageresource.com/dhtml/csstut1.htm

Assessing yourself

Think about the work you have done as you worked through this book.
Put a tick next to the sentences below that describe what you have done.

Level 4

I planned and created some web pages suitable for the target audience ☐

I added suitable text and images to my web pages ☐

I created hyperlinks to join my web pages together ☐

I evaluated my web pages to check that they met the needs of the target audience ☐

I described how my web pages might be improved ☐

Level 5

I planned and created some web pages suitable for a range of different users ☐

I added suitable text and images to my web pages and gave some
reasons for the choices I made ☐

I evaluated my web pages to check that they met the needs of a range of different users ☐

Level 6

I used feedback from users to improve my web pages ☐

Index